Praise f

An intimate, thoughtful and reflective series of prose following a young woman's journey through love, loss and life. While she finds herself through these words, may you also find yourself, and feel a little less alone.

~ *Caitlin*

Some artists remind you that words can be beautiful, and Alexandra is one of these artists. Behind her beautiful language is raw emotion and startling realism. Poems such as *It's 4 o'clock on a Saturday* follow thought patterns that feel so right you forget they're not your own, while *You're in good company* perfectly encapsulates how I feel after I visit her or other good friends, however rare it is nowadays. This is nothing short of an art collection, candidly demonstrating the beauty of being vulnerable, as she delicately writes in *I know what I want for my daughter*.

~ *Krista*

We are invited into Alexandra's most intimate thoughts, welcomed by her vulnerability, and comforted by her courage. Her incredibly personal tale is one I believe we can all relate to. As I read her words I saw myself; grieving on one page, and beaming with hope on the next. As pains of memories past came to the surface, I was comforted by her gentle words. With the flip of every page I am reminded that *my truth, I've learned - is growing and shaping*. That no matter the distance, we can find our way back home. That above all else, we must look within and meet our own souls with kindness. Keep this collection by your bedside, and close to your heart. No matter the pain, I know you will find hope in her poetry.

~ *Leen*

I was at an open-door event in early 2020, when an energetic young lady approached me, and we started to chat. Wow, I remember thinking to myself. I wish I was as confident as her. Since then, and to this day, she continues to inspire me with her independence, strength and resilience.

Here I am now, sipping my morning coffee, and my first impression upon reading her collection is, I like it. I really, really like it. It feels like an old soul in a young body. I am so happy for her. She has figured it out early; it starts with me, it is what I make it to be, I do matter, my love matters, and I choose to love myself even in times of wonder and pain. I would say these poems are a monument of self worth. Every girl who doubts herself should read this collection.

I want to share these lines with my daughter, my nieces, my goddaughters, every woman in fact:

> *I'll give her this one gift*
> *as the only reminder either of us need*
> *to wait for the man*
> *who will love the beauty within me*

I can now see how Alexandra's experiences and inner work have shaped her into the young, confident lady who once started a chat with me.

~ Madara

Letters ^{to} Myself

Alexandra Mireanu

Dear Sunita,

I hope this poetry uplifts & inspires you
to be more of who you are ♡

Love,
   Alexandra

Dec 2022

Edited by Vanessa Mainella, with supervision by Shelly Zevlever

Book Design by Reilly Ballantyne

ISBN 978-1-7778519-1-0 (paperback)
ISBN 978-1-7778519-0-3 (ebook)

Plume Press is an imprint of Plume,
a product of The Soap Box Press

Plume
Toronto, Ontario
www.plumepress.com

Table of Contents

A Foreword

At first, I wasn't sure how to approach writing this. I've never written a foreword before, and I didn't want to disappoint. As I began reading this collection though, I was relieved to find it well-written, and I instantly resonated with so many ideas within these pages.

About a decade ago, I taught Alexandra in my highschool English class. I always knew she was very special. Her skill and talent for creative writing, and literature analysis, shined through our discussions and her essays on works such as King Lear and The Kite Runner. Alexandra has always had a profound way of seeing things, offering a perspective far beyond her years. Her ability to analyze and capture raw emotions is abundantly clear in this collection. Here, as readers, we are provided an opportunity to crawl into Alexandra's heart and mind. With a glimpse into her private life as she shares her ponderings and meanderings on love and relationships, pain and heartache, and her coming-of-age, she harnesses the challenges life presents her to grow and persevere.

With a heightened sense of understanding, Alexandra comes to terms with her grappling self-doubt. She represents a battle many women face with their worth as we struggle to recognize our value and believe in ourselves. As women we often readily calculate our worth based on how others see us. Alexandra also gives testimony to the objectification women may feel in their lives. In her poem *I'm learning to be human*, we see her rejection of the societal implications that a woman's role lies within the institution of marriage, and how she chooses to take a more holistic path towards self-acceptance, self-empowerment and self-love. We see a pivotal shift at the core of her writing as she chooses this path, describing the sheer confidence and joy this decision brings her. She finally knows her own worth and doesn't look for another to define it to her.

We are well introduced to Alexandra's past relationships and the loves that touched her heart along the way. Her accounts reveal the initial infatuation, joy and excitement that inevitably come with young love. All elation though eventually subsides, and her words reveal a painful emptiness as she feels disappointed once again in what she's found. She yearns for more connection, acknowledgment, and depth in her relationships, and is finally able to recognize the dangers in needing another person to feel fulfilled. It is only after we go through such trials and learn to love ourselves, that we can cultivate love that truly contributes to our life.

There are also accounts that connect us to Alexandra's upbringing. The connection between her own relationships in adulthood and those with her family is done quite purposefully. Each and every one of us is shaped by the dynamics we see within our family. Our expectations and the choices we make are largely connected by the narratives we learn as children, positive or otherwise. Alexandra provides us a unique glimpse into her own mother's difficulty to see her self-worth and natural beauty. We begin to understand the underlying narrative that was passed down to her. From a young age, her value and worth felt dependent on others' acceptance and expression of love towards her. As she became a woman in her own right, this evidently translated into the eyes of the men she loved. Indeed, only once we are able to let go of these learned self-limiting beliefs, can we truly believe in our own worth. As she reminds us in her poem, *Love like you would love a flower*:

> *don't stifle your growth for too long*
> *in any one place*
> *keep growing*
> *reaching*
> *before you dry up*
> *and it's too late*

Alexandra brilliantly reveals her truth on these pages, paying homage to the challenges that shaped her. This collection provides a phenomenal testimony for any young man or woman learning to grow in their own skin. She welcomes us to question the lessons we learn and the narratives we absorb as young boys and girls; to unravel our inner truth, re-discover our worth, and make space for the love we deserve. Only then can we find joy within ourselves and experience the joy we truly desire in the relationships around us.

Rebecca Summers
August 8, 2021

My Gift to You

I still remember the sound of his voice, even though it's been years since I last heard it. My grandfather's handwritten letters and poems remain safely tucked away in my nightstand drawer. Once in a blue moon, I open this drawer to remember his words of consolation, for his life coming to a close. The art of writing brought him great solace. For the same reason he wrote his last words, I sit here writing mine.

These poems weren't written for you, they were written for me. As a child I would eagerly begin a new journal, but each time it would be left behind. Unfinished. This collection is no different. It is a collection of the journals I kept through love and loss, rebuilding a life, exploring sexuality, and discovering what it feels like to be free. This collection is a testament that I can do anything if my heart is present and my mind doesn't interfere. Mistakes happen when we let fear decide, when we let fear choose for us. Yet even for the incredibly difficult times I've written about here, I don't regret a single thing.

While everything you are about to read has already passed, the memories they conjure are so vivid and profound, I carry them with me wherever I go. There are lines I've pondered deeply and re-written numerous times, while there are entire entries that compellingly flowed out of me with no regard for time, or place, or hesitation.

Time after time I have found solace in the written word even when I am at a loss for what to say out loud. Heightened emotions are a wonderful thing for an artist. They move us to act, to create, to express how we feel in an attempt to understand our human experience. Writing is a means of returning to oneself and remembering that you are home.

Wherever you go, there you are. This is my gift to you.

Alexandra Mireanu
June 20, 2021

Letters ^{to} Myself

Self-Worth

Darling
you are my light
you are who I run to every time

Love yourself a little wilder
than you love anyone else
goodness knows
you deserve it

Today I am reminded
that all I want
and what is to come
is undecided

I am learning to thrive
on what is within

by the swing of a pendulum
how happy I am
for where I have been

I want to rejoice
in this present state
feel grateful for every moment
and welcome every lesson

Believe in me
when I confess
my love and devotion
to the art of living

at last
I'm no longer holding my breath

I'm learning to be human
I don't need a white dress
makeup
or a flight of stairs
I'm looking within myself
at the love I possess
filling my own empty spaces
painting a canvas
learning to love the phases
places
I find myself

embracing the changes
in a silence all too rare
taking strides
setting the pace
awaking in disbelief
the morning of each day
learning to accept
where I have been
and who I am

Locks of gold
elegantly sway in the breeze
protecting this loving heart
and mind that thinks

with the lips of a goddess
I speak
I'm worth more
than anything you could offer me

the curvatures of my body
plump and tempting
will capture you
as your eyes longingly stare
imagining what is underneath

Few will understand
the sense of calm that comes
from knowing your heart
is safe
in your own respect
there's a beauty in such peace
that cannot be found
in the eyes
body or heart
of another man

When they call me beautiful
I always reply *I know*
to all the sides of my body and soul

I had to learn how to love myself
this is what happens when you have no example
for how a woman recognizes beauty in herself

I now realize
the injustice men will serve
if I look to them to define my worth

remember
some men just want their way
with another pretty face
and as I write this now
I'm teaching my mother too
even if it's the only way I can repay her
for patiently raising me
and never quieting my glow

I'll give her this one gift
as the only reminder either of us need
to wait for the man
who will love the beauty within me

A feeling takes what meaning
we choose to let it bear
a tear that is shed
is pleading to be felt

a touch on your skin reminds you
of the wondrous body
you are in

a deep hope for love
does not undermine your self worth
you are worthy and loved
wholly by how you feel
within

love from your heart
that you carry in each step
is the truth you seek
to understand
and believe that *you*
can conquer every fear
it's all you need
to come home to yourself

Love like you would love a flower

water
nurture
self-expose your skin to the sun
then when the rain comes
let it all pour down

don't stifle your growth
for too long
in any one place
keep growing
reaching
before you dry up
and it's too late

They say love is blind
to be faithful
you must believe in something kind

well I believe in my soul
in these words there are
innumerable worlds
aware of a love
with no end in sight
by the depth I feel
in my own presence
amidst this peaceful twilight

I believe in what you believe
because I believe in you
I don't need proof
or reassurance
that what you believe to be true
is true
because you believe in it
and I believe in you

Your beauty
doesn't deserve to live
in the shadow
of another's jealousy

Lessons Learned

Loneliness makes the heart grow fonder
more desperate
desolate
seemingly beyond repair

fondness captures your spirit's freedom
and strips you bare
the day your love is not returned

sadness overflows
somehow calming your soul
and at last you feel at home

but never the same
never a feeling of being safe
from the intoxication of young love

Your hand rests warmly on my back
as we walk through this breeze
I lock my fingers in yours
while you hold my frame
tenderly

please
continue to carry me
no matter how coldly
I give myself to you

There stood a skeleton of a man
long forgotten behind this door
his few belongings in the corner
of a room vastly bare

for a dream in long-held hope
here lay proof that any fruition
remained scarce

it was undoubtedly easier
to envision our future
yesterday

I remember the days
I loved foolishly
giving my heart away
to a boy I believed would be a good man
for the children I wanted to carry
until the days I was waiting for change
became too commonplace
through a storm
weathering my soul
I learned to navigate loss on my own

I stayed and fought because I believe in love
slowly I started to see
I was worthy of more
I knew the kind of love I wanted to feel

Accepting what remained unknown
on the other side of my old apartment door
I packed my things
uprooted the life I had lived for 4 years
and found my way back home

He wrapped his arm around my waist
effortlessly I felt all those butterflies

I warned you I would stray
but did you listen?

you couldn't hear
through your indifference
drowning out all the beauty
you could have in this life

I denied you repeatedly
because a woman needs to feel loved
before she'll give you her body
she can't be claimed
but she doesn't deserve to walk alone either

so the next time she stands before you
love her like the sun

Running wild in an open field
feeling myself defy gravity
becoming part of a new family
while estranged from my own

losing my best friend on a technicality
repairing relationships broken long ago
caring for a man despite imminent danger
being abandoned in a city not my own

turning to strangers for unfound guidance
almost suffocating from feeling anxious
falling unconscious in a foreign country
nearly changing my name to his

breaking the rules of infidelity
savouring sex like it was the answer
uncovering truths I wish I didn't know

A bachelor of the arts
poised
regressed
treading the water
of this newfound romance

in his asking
I answered
our burning desires

he spoke
as I prayed
at ungodly hours

if I could believe
his words as true
they would say an effortless
I
love
you

but he hardly knew
he left a soul behind
with scars undone
by his point of view

Oh what I didn't know
sitting on my kitchen floor
talking to the open air
asking questions between heavy breaths

the room too crowded
demanding answers
I wouldn't understand

It's 4 o'clock on a Saturday
by the sun reflecting
on this hardwood floor
I see the shadow of a hand and smile
knowing it's my own

I forgot what it's like
spending days without talking
to anyone
I once thrived in the ecstasy
that comes from living
unchained by time
by the scars brought upon me

pretending tomorrow did not matter
as much as the day ahead

well, that became a fallacy
the night you said
you loved everything about me
but after years of misguidance
the same words wouldn't come
until you kissed me
and by the touch of our lips
we drifted into a dream

you didn't speak to me this Saturday
seemingly going your separate way
I waited to see
what you would decide
when I placed no expectation
and put on a brave face

as most days
you surprised me
here I was hoping
you would come

once you stood there I felt lost
I still don't expect you to understand
why I needed you there

caught in my emotions
my eyes would frantically dart
until they met your gaze
and the tears slowly came
when you asked if I was going to be okay

after a pause
I answered
then I wrote this poem
sitting by the sun

I once read love is a choice
now there are days when I ask why
why does love feel hard sometimes?

when I look into your eyes
mine confess
how deeply I believe in us
while your eyes reveal everything else

I drive home at the end of the day
and all I see in passing
somehow brings me back to you

I will always want to be closer
to the man I love

I've been here before
though this time I'm less alone

I thought I would have more time
to look into your eyes

I thought you believed in me
for the words I spoke

no one knows what you said
yet here I am wondering
if it might be true

how your feelings became fickle
fleeting beneath the stars

now under the moon
I look up to look at you

You're still in my dreams
this morning I woke up with you in my head
thinking how precious our time was
from the hourglass looking in

no one could have guessed
a love like ours could be

lately I've been trying to let go
of the choice I made

cutting you off and moving on
was it a mistake?

for months distance kept us apart
and I vowed I would give us a chance
the first chance I got
I care for you as deeply as I once cared for someone else
but now you are just another dream
I lost

Love Echoes

In your eyes I look
searching
your gaze reassures me
I am enough
we deserve everything love is

we were never too much

I cannot put into words
how it feels
how I've yearned
to hear you say these words

to the moon
to the sun
through any storm
I will be there

You're in good company
when you feel a smile
laying across your face
after you've spent the day
with an old friend

your heart overflows
in the space you've shared
the voices in your head
reminding you it's okay

friendship is rare
in a world that sometimes shakes
and buckles you at the knees

under a pressure all-knowing
this is the one place
where you are accepted as you are
embraced and loved
for just being alive

that's what I've come
to greatly appreciate

You make me want to believe
the love stories I read
about how two people
can happily be

my worth you've never questioned
my heart always treated
with utmost affection
my fears and doubts relieved
each time I find my way back
to myself and my lessons

your embrace lingers
with each passing day
and what is left unspoken
I profoundly hear you say

as the roar of a burning fire
through your actions
it's all becoming clear

I can now believe in happy endings
and beginnings
and journeys through time
I can see one day
what my life might be like
because of the love you've shown me
since our first time

With each new encounter
in love I find
something worth celebrating
if only for a moment in time

I don't hear a word you're saying
as I admire in awe
the man you are

you tell me stories of the pleiades
how a constellation came to be
what are the chances of us meeting?

it's easy to fathom what this could be

I often stop to think
how this is all possible
even now, in the midst of it
you are always so sure of me

Thank you for giving me
your time and trust
it feels as though
you take great care with love

you look to me and ask
what do you want?
no man before you
has shown me this
without the expectation
of a destination
to fuel his own afflictions

we'll sit and talk for hours
on fears and predispositions
until our eyes sparkle
from love's ammunition
and we are too tired
to continue this conversation

we embrace and retrace
the clarity we've gained
seeing kindness and acceptance
across the other's face

I knew I was safe
by the presence of a hand
guiding my back gently forward

by his kindness
the kindest of hearts

by the softness in his eyes
how he looked at me
as though captivated at first sight
every time

tints of feelings
echoing in his voice
always reminding me
to be who I am

It was assumed we would be
rocking our tent
as the others did
shamelessly

but we only came here to rest

I kissed his forehead
he kissed my hand
our fingers held on dearly in comfort
as we drifted into dreams
cheek to cheek

When I say I love you
its because it's true
when you let me in and let me hold you
I am home
and no matter where I go
there's no place as wonderful as this
knowing my touch
my embrace
has captured your world

Let's swim in each other's waves
laugh at the end of each day
disfigure our bodies as they wrap
in and out
let's fall madly
until we hit the ground running
for more precious moments in this life

Between skinned sheets
we couldn't help but stare
deep in disbelief
our eyes dancing in the act

all I ask is that you
paint me with your kisses
breathe in my breath
the way my father first kissed my mother
blazed in candlelight

with the embrace of an empire
we knew anything could happen

and then the moment passes

I'll stare at the city skyline
glance up at floating clouds
breath in this breeze
as it whistles through the trees
admiring all of these elements
only to remember you

I would go back in time
try to rectify every decision I made
to be a better woman for you

I would go back in time
to the days when you felt most alone
and reach my hand out to you

I would go back in time
to every time you felt unloved
and hold you tight

I would go back in time
to all the years I didn't know you
and tell you I love you

I would go back in time
to when you were a boy
just to see you smile

The Truth About Home

Their pictures are kept
in a hand-carved wooden box
and on my wrist you'll always find
the infinity sign
as reminders for how frail
and temporary
all this really is

My grandmother wed, raising two kids
by age twenty-four
living a life of class and charm
born in the countryside
on the side of a hill
overlooking the town my mother's dad is from

she smiled and wept
with a fire in her eyes
reminiscing at the time
her daughter said goodbye
words surprisingly unreal
to describe the overwhelming compassion I feel
for the strongest woman I've known my whole life

she has always loved me unconditionally
showing a strength
she rarely knew she carried

she was my first home
the place I was brought to
after being brought into this world

now she lives there on her own
my beautiful loving Maria

Dear grandfather
thank you for the times your photograph
came in handy

for remembering

reminding me
what hope feels like

in the look in your eyes
I swear I can see you smile
despite all you've survived

He asked to take a photograph
as we drove down our sunny lane

it seems silly now
to think how I hesitate
little did I know
that would be the last time
I see my grandfather's face
standing outside his house
hand in hand
waving goodbye and
blowing me kisses
the way Romanians do

I still see it all
as though it was yesterday
even though it's been a year
since he passed away
and three years since
I last saw my grandmother's grace

in a few short months
I'll be walking down the same sunny lane
on the street I first knew

She looked in my eyes
longer than any woman
or child of mine
having me believe in kindness
my ancestors were never shown

age sprinkled on her face
a voice of spirit and grace
soft
quiet in strength

I fall into his grave
hoping the darkness will save
my dreams from crumbling

under me
around me
I feel the earth

her warmth encapsulating
my tears and fears
slowly drifting away

I walk out quietly
touching every heart in that family

I outgrew him unintentionally
while you - unbeknownst to me
continued to love me from afar

telling him everything I knew to be true
and needed to hear

standing up for my honour
simply because you believe in me

sparing my spirit
graciously

preserving the air I breathe

On this red couch
where you first tried to
I sit wondering
if I'm ready

between tears and broken dreams
markings on the stove-top
still glare up at me

I didn't know whether to stay or go
my emotions running amok
between these light yellow walls

will I find the courage to get out
before the anger worsens?

if only I had a mantelpiece
on which to lay down these feelings
would they even be worthy
of being read, comprehended
cherished by the man who once knew me?

here I am again
contemplating a most trying time
of repression and self-neglect

the young night before me
seeking permission to change my mind
I glide across the house
pick up my mother's rustic leather jacket
and walk out

Up in the attic
I sit on a ledge
overlooking a garden
lovelier than the rest

surrounded by keepsakes
suitcases that once roamed
brightly coloured tapestries
people in photographs
I don't know

days were long at four years of age
displaced by my mother
who lived a continent away

dust having settled
coating all that remains

I know what I want for my daughter

a love that teaches her
she is lovable

a love that shows her
the beauty of being vulnerable

a love that gives her courage
to love another

Thank you for loving me
you were my first home
the years were good to you
for the long life you had
your wife cared for you
like no one else

I was astray and abroad
more than I came to visit
you are in almost every thought
every breath
every song I hear and listen

I didn't know you all that well
but you'll be in my heart forever

sometimes I cry
thinking about coming home
to a place that no longer holds you

on a day I knew would come
I no longer heard you
though I can still replay
the sound of your voice
by our last conversation
as familiar as rain
before embarking on a journey
seeking the soul of Asia to serve me
not knowing I was saying goodbye already

I've heard the walk up the hill is the hardest
to relive and recount
each painfully beautiful memory
with every step in honesty

I have yet to show my face
in my hometown
where you now lay to rest

nothing could possibly prepare me
yet I know the day will come
I just don't know when

Wandering

Time will pass anyway
even on a rainy day
what seems so far away
is already approaching

so rest and rejoice
for this life in passing
as nothing is here to stay

not even your pain

We are stardust
matter that has been transformed
within the universe
into beings
rebuilt from the sky
crashing down to earth
matter
re-engineered by generations
to become us

we learned to seek
grow, guide, fly
to speak, read, write

we were given life
we knew instinctively
how to survive
but we chose to thrive

we came from this earth
we need to breathe

we were given life
and look at all we have seen
all we have achieved

to those we love
and those we distaste
we are all children of the same matter
and all matter in the milky way

I walk these streets
look at these humans
whom I don't know
who don't meet

I hope my heart
will be spared
of the turmoils
of unrequited love
of the indecencies
a lack of humanity
can bring to a person's life

I see children skating
men in ragged clothes
living on the street floor
waiting
I hope these sights
don't encompass all there is to see

I hope
I want to believe

It has always been clear
as humans
we share a temporary existence
witnessed in fragments
intoxicated by the ridicule
of our ancestors
or creatures of the divine
which are arguably
a man's distraction
in understanding
his own reason for being alive

Monuments tower over us
in our golden life and glory years
the sky seems far yet near
as I lay without any stars
staring at the vastness
of this dark
wondering how
with all this space
we have managed to trade
peace and tranquility
for brighter nights
and darker days

I walk until my neck aches
from the force of gravity
watchful of the streets
with probing eyes
and eager ears

figurines on the sidewalk
a woman with orange locks of hair
a man walking with a cup
smiling to himself
a bookshop filled with more people
than the street
a walk in solidarity
for an insomniac's bite to eat

we sit and drink and speak
on our love for inhibitions
and how we've managed to stray
from this world's addictions

staring at the mountain of food on our plates
the price of living in Toronto
our city and home
discussing our favourite times to date

so rarely we possess the necessary strength
to meet a week's working demands
yet we remain unabiding citizens
on the act of rest
a test we fail above all else
as we desperately search for the great escape

If life was a dream
I wonder how different we would be
knowing we have an opportunity
to create our reality

I wonder how we would smile
knowing we are beautiful
by how we share ourselves
and care

if only we knew
to embrace love in spite of fear
realizing its strength lies in self-doubt
and that the sooner we act
the easier it is to overcome

There is truth in every word
in every sound
however discrete

our souls
alone they may be
but it is our choice
to not let them become empty

our clothes
keep us warm
but cannot save us from ourselves

no soul should be left behind
our presence matters
we deserve to be held
in the company of those we cherish

A great calm
will sweep this nation
when we help our neighbor
in hope of curing starvation

of the heart, mind and spirit
there's plenty to give in theory

but alas
many of us choose
a lonelier route
to the same destination

What is difficult to express
will often possess
a special place in your heart

these roots in you
need water to flow through
if you wish to let them grow

there is a fear I've seen
between these sheets
of unfulfilled dreams
to which I want to speak

walk down the street
really look at everyone I meet
there's love and kindness to be shared here

before the night falls
and the day reappears

I lost you in the crowd
you crossed a corner
not wanting to be found
left on my own
in a city I didn't know
with no map or change
no place to call home

I sat on the steps of an ice cream shop
a traveler soon came to me with kind words
between my tears I drank the water he handed me
and was finally able to stop

I began walking on my own
unsure of where to go
it felt so strange
to be in the city of the Duomo

in a piazza with an abandoned fountain
my spirit bare of skin and clothes
standing tall I looked up
at what we were all here for

for the first and final hour
lying awake in a sweeping calm
I listened to you proclaim
how nothing had been the same
the day I was gone

It's you they worship
as you gaze from the sky
truth be told
I am unsure if I believe
the story of how you die

your love for them is beautiful and kind
but as a child of the divine
all I can believe in clarity
is how I was once born
in a home, naturally

I can breathe and speak
I can choose what I believe

I believe I can foster love
for these delicate parts of me

I believe I can love another
another soul unique to my own
and live with them in harmony
or what you may call destiny

I can hear the lioness within
roar
knowing I have everything I need

Observations in the Wild

Trees whistle in the breeze
grass stands tall
rocks scrap my feet

the discomfort of being
belongs to me
I will continue to choose
to freeze in time
to breathe among the trees
for I know tomorrow may not be

There is a bird
now two
chasing each other in the sky
oh my, what a sight
what beauty young love sounds like

a force to be reckoned with
a force to crave

The sun is gone
the sky is near
the sights are bright and shining clear
as I travel through the streets
I wonder how I'm really here

the road is frantic
but I am centered
as air rushes through me

I recognize that being here is courageous

I trust in him, I trust in us
that we have not mistaken
our path for a vacation

I would rather fall into the rain
than feel myself forever
in mild sorrow

precipitating
waiting for a storm
that may never come

The air, my breath
my view has shaken

no food, no light
can undo these realizations

my truth, I've learned
is growing and shaping

who I am
how I am
how I wish to be

Wildlife is mystifying
with no creatures in sight
I can hear them all
the birds, crickets and snakes
I wish I knew how to fully appreciate
all that nature has to offer

each new ecosystem I encounter
reminds me of my limited line of sight
I feel small yet strong
incapable of surrendering to the wild

a part of me at peace in the loneliness

a part of me set free

The sky is clear
as far as the eye can see
the fog has lifted
the light is here
the day is young
the night was not
afraid of what I may have done
afraid of today I am not

to be hurt and loved
to be here
to feel

I am aware I can choose
which feelings guide me

Upside down the flower lays
behaving as though it has rained
the heat exhausting all that remains
the only temperament this place has faced
a climate few could have survived
yet here a flower lays
in the place where it never rains

About the Author

As an avid reader, competitive dancer, and professionally trained pianist, Alexandra Mireanu has been immersed in the arts her entire life. In her teens, she taught piano and music theory to children, even to those her own age. Born in Suceava, Romania, she spent her childhood summers with her grandparents while tending to her formal education in Canada during the school year. She fell in love with language and literature in large part through her unique bilingual upbringing.

Alexandra discovered an insatiable desire for writing poetry while travelling through Southeast Asia in 2019. This is her debut poetry collection. It contains the original poems she wrote on her travels and encompasses her journey to the ripe age of 25.

In 2021, Alexandra completed Life Stories, a memoir writing course through the University of Toronto. She also joined a Toronto-based writing group for young, aspiring creatives. As an emerging memoirist and essayist, she hopes to publish collections of creative nonfiction someday.

For more information about the author Alexandra Mireanu,
please visit alexandramireanu.weebly.com